BUTTERFLIES OF VERMONT
AND THEIR HOST PLANTS

KATE TAYLOR

This edition published in 2025 by
Trafalgar Square Books
The Stable Book Group, Brooklyn, New York

Copyright © 2024, 2025 Kate Taylor

All rights reserved. No part of this book may be reproduced, by any means, without written permission of the publisher, except by a reviewer quoting brief excerpts for a review in a magazine, newspaper, or website.

Disclaimer of Liability
The author and publisher shall have neither liability nor responsibility to any person or entity with respect to any loss or damage caused or alleged to be caused directly or indirectly by the information contained in this book. While the book is as accurate as the author can make it, there may be errors, omissions, and inaccuracies.

Trafalgar Square Books certifies that the content in this book was generated by a human expert on the subject, and the content was edited, fact-checked, and proofread by human publishing specialists. TSB does not publish books generated by artificial intelligence (AI).

Library of Congress Control Number: 2025938184
ISBN: 9781646013098

All photographs by Kate Taylor except as indicated in the Acknowledgments.

Book interior and cover design byRM Didier

Typeface: Myriad
Printed in the United States of America
10 9 8 7 6 5 4 3 2 1

For Char, 'cause *you* are the BEST

CONTENTS

Preface vii

Introduction 1

What Is a Butterfly? 2

BUTTERFLY FAMILIES 6–44

Swallowtails (*Papilionidae*) 6

Brushfoots (*Nymphalidae*) 8

Gossamerwings (*Lycaenidae*) 24

Whites and Yellows (*Pieridae*) 31

Skippers (*Hesperiidae*) 34

Host Plants 45

Making a Difference 52

At a Glance 54

Resources 66

Acknowledgments 67

Index 68

Baltimore Checkerspot

Black Swallowtail

PREFACE

During the COVID lock-down I took a course on identifying butterflies and I fell in love. I started almost daily butterfly walks. I planted a butterfly garden, then another. I began mowing paths instead of a lawn. Now, when not out looking for butterflies, I battle invasive plants that are crowding out butterfly host plants. On my walks I look closely at the plants and animals around me, becoming more deeply engaged with this beautiful world we seem intent on destroying.

I want to save the tiny animals that I see on my walks. I want Hairstreaks to abound and Monarchs to flourish. I want to know that the Brown Elfin I saw this summer won't be the last one I see. These insects need our help. I may not be able to help polar bears or African elephants, but I can plant a garden that will welcome butterflies and give them a place to live.

My hope is that this guide will inspire you to take a second and third look at the butterflies around you. May you too fall in love with them and want to help them survive.

In this guide I emphasize the butterflies you are most likely to see in your Vermont wanderings. I hope you find many rare and beautiful exceptions, but since that is by definition unlikely, I felt that focusing on the common locals would give you the most useful information.

You can find the conservation status of all Vermont Butterflies on page 53, but the main entries are the butterflies you are likely to see when you spend time in the field.

Black Swallowtail (left) Crescent (right).

Atlantis (left) and Great Spangled (right) Fritillaries.

Who knows, maybe that distant leaf is actually a butterfly.

INTRODUCTION

Differentiating one butterfly from another can be as easy as glancing at its color and posture, or it can require close study. Usually it falls somewhere in between.

Rather than starting by trying to distinguish the difficult butterflies like Fritillaries or Grass Skippers, I recommend identifying the different families. Learn to distinguish a Skipper from a Fritillary, then learn to tell the Great Spangled Fritillary from the Atlantis Fritillary or a Pecks Skipper from a Hobomok Skipper.

In Vermont there are five butterfly families. They are the Brushfoots (*Nymphalidae*), Gossamerwings (*Lycaenidae*), Skippers (*Hesperiidae*), Swallowtails (*Papilionidae*), and Whites and Yellows (*Pieridae*). We don't have the sixth family of butterflies, the Metalmarks (*Riodinidae*) in Vermont.

Within each family are further breakdowns into subfamilies, genera (singular, genus) and species, but placing a butterfly into its family is a good way to learn general butterfly shapes and habits. From there you can learn other ways to group similar butterflies before trying to tackle more difficult species identifications.

Learn to ask yourself some questions: What are the main colors? How large is it? Does it rest with wings open or closed? What is the habitat and time of year? Does its behavior suggest a species? What family do you think it belongs to?

Butterflies can be busy, flitting here and there, or they can be still as a stone. Heading to the correct habitat is the first step in finding them, but it helps to have an idea how to search. We are used to seeing what is large and obvious. It may take a while to see the small and unobtrusive. Teach yourself to take a second look at that shadow or flicker of movement.

WHAT IS A BUTTERFLY?

Butterflies are winged insects in the order *Lepidoptera*. All plants and animals identified by science are given a scientific name and classification. The name is usually based on Latin or Greek roots and prevents confusion when scientists speak different languages, or when an animal has more than one common name. The classification identifies where the plant or animal fits within the tree of life.

Cats and butterflies are both animals in the kingdom *Animalia* (animals), so they share the characteristics specific to the kingdom of animals. Since this is a general category, the shared characteristics are also general. For example, all animals have a nervous system.

Once you get down to deeper levels of classification, the shared characteristics become more specific. Butterflies are insects, so, like all insects, they have a head, thorax, and abdomen, plus six legs and a pair of antennae. Within the class *Insecta,* butterflies branch further into the order *Lepidoptera,* which includes moths. Specifically, these are winged insects with scaled bodies. These microscopic scales, and the way they reflect and refract light, are responsible for the beautiful colors of moths and butterflies.

Within the order *Lepidoptera,* we get to the six families of butterflies, of which Vermont sees five as described earlier. Within each of these families are different traits which can help identify a butterfly. For instance, Skippers tend to be small with quick erratic flight, while Swallowtails are large and more likely to soar. Learning the distinctions between families is a great way to start identifying butterflies. Beyond families are subfamilies, genera, and then species. A few species are nearly impossible to distinguish and I've grouped these into genera since most enthusiasts don't travel with a microscope.

Like many insects, butterflies undergo full metamorphosis, meaning they fully change shape during their lives. A female butterfly can lay from one to hundreds of eggs at a time, depending on the species. The eggs hatch and the larvae (caterpillars) emerge.

Caterpillars have a reputation for being pests, but they are truly marvelous creatures. Their only job in life is to eat and they do their job well. A few species harm plants, but the majority are harmless to human interests. Before you kill a caterpillar, consider whether it is actually doing harm or if it might be an endangered butterfly that needs all the help it can get.

Regardless of species, caterpillars are eating machines. They eat until they no longer fit into their body, then they molt. Their skin splits and they wiggle out, with a fresh new body that is more or less similar to the one they just abandoned. Each new body is called an instar. Different species have different numbers of instars, but five is common. The first instar is minuscule. As they molt, the instars often change; some caterpillars grow horns, some eyespots, an the Monarch will become yellow, white, and black.

An egg (upper left) and a first instar Monarch caterpillar (circled) next to a pencil for size comparison.

Caterpillars eat so much because they need enough energy to pupate, the process that begins their transformation into butterflies. Unlike most moths, butterflies don't make a silk cocoon to surround their body. A cocoon is a external covering made to protect an insect's body. You can remove the pupa, the insect itself, from the cocoon.

Cecropia moth cocoon and pupa.

Butterflies, in contrast, form a chrysalis, which is part of their body. Inside the chrysalis, the caterpillar, now called a pupa, dissolves into undifferentiated cells which will reform as new body parts. Some of the caterpillar retains its old form—for instance, the caterpillar legs form the foundation for the butterfly's legs—but much of the change happens from the cellular level on up.

Baltimore Checkerspot chrysalis.

The entire process can occur in as little as two weeks, or it can take months. For species who overwinter, the animal goes into diapause, a low energy state similar to hibernation. In this case, all activity ceases until the weather, the amount of light, or some other signal tells the butterfly it is time to emerge (called eclosing).

As the time comes for the butterfly to eclose, the chrysalis may change color and you can begin to see the form of an adult butterfly beneath. Eventually the butterfly will break through the chrysalis into its final form. It spreads its wings and rests until it is ready for its first flight. Then off into the world it goes as a fully formed adult butterfly.

Basic Butterfly Glossary

Abdomen — rear part of the body, behind the thorax
Antenna — long, slender, sensory organs attached to the head
Antenna club — the end of the antenna
Chrysalis — the form a butterfly takes as it morphs from caterpillar to adult butterfly, often hanging from a thread on its host plant
Costal margin (costa) — leading edge of forewing
Basal band — band on the wing closer to the body than the median band, used to define coloration (eg: black stripe through basal band)
Fringe — fine ends of wingtips
FW — forewing
HW — hindwing
Larva — caterpillar stage of a butterfly (plural larvae)
Margin — edge of wing
Median band (mb) — center of wing
Palps — segmented appendages near the mouth, thought to be taste sensors
Postmedian (pm) — past the middle of the wing away from the body
Proboscis — hollow, tongue-like structure used for sucking up nectar
Puddling — when butterflies congregate near a mud puddle or wet area to search for nutrients
Pupa — the intermediate stage of a butterfly between caterpillar and adult butterfly; in butterflies the pupa is usually called a chrysalis
Thorax — body behind the head, where wings and legs are attached
Trailing margin — bottom edge of wing
Submarginal (sm) — area just inside the furthest edge of the wing

Butterfly Sizes

Tiny: ¾"–1" (20 – 25mm)

Small (Sm): 1" – 1⅜" (25 – 35mm)

Medium (Med): ⅜" – 2" (35 – 50mm)

Large (L): 2"– 2¾" (50 – 70mm)

Extra Large (XL): over 2¾" (over 70mm)

Parts of the Butterfly

SWALLOWTAILS (*PAPILIONIDAE*)

Swallowtails are large butterflies, named for the "tails" on their hindwings. There are around 30 species in North America, although most of them live in the South. Their large size and bright coloring make them easy to spot.

Swallowtails tend to beat their wings relatively slowly compared with the sometimes frenetic flapping of other butterflies but they can move rapidly and often soar across meadows and among treetops. Once you start to notice them you'll begin to see them all over.

Our two common Swallowtails are the Canadian Tiger Swallowtail (*Papilio canadensis*) and the Black Swallowtail (*Papilio polyxenes*) but several others can occasionally be seen in our area. These include the Eastern Tiger Swallowtail (*Papilio glaucus*), the Giant Swallowtail (*Papilio cresphontes*), the Spicebush Swallowtail (*Papilio triolus*), and the Pipevine Swallowtail (*Battus philenor*).

The Canadian and Eastern Tiger Swallowtails often interbreed, making them hard to differentiate (I suspect a plot among butterflies to create confusion in aspiring Lepidopterists).

— Black Swallowtail (*Papilio polyxenes*) —

(XL)

Flies May–Oct

Adults nectar on many flowers, including milkweed and clover.

Host plants are members of the Parsley family including carrot, fennel, and Queen Anne's Lace.

The Black Swallowtail is dark black above with yellow spots forming a band along the wing margins and a band of blue with orange spots on the lower HW. Females have a row of yellow spots as well as a blue band along their hindwings. They are found in a variety of open areas, especially disturbed habitats, including fields, gardens, and roadsides.

KATE TAYLOR

— Canadian Tiger Swallowtail (*Papilio canadensis*) —

(XL)

Flies May–
Mid July

Adults nectar on many flowers.

Host plants include birch, aspen, and cherry.

These large butterflies like to soar and perch. Canadian and Eastern Tiger Swallowtails look similar and often hybridize. Trying to distinguish them in the field is difficult. In Vermont, the Canadian Tiger is much more common. They live in many habitats and can be found throughout the state. They like deciduous and mixed woods and edges.

— Eastern Giant Swallowtail (*Papilio cresphontes*) —

(XL)

Flies April–Oct

Adults nectar on many flowers including goldenrods and milkweeds.

Host plants are mainly citrus, but also prickly ash, among others.

The Giant Swallowtails can only overwinter in the deep South, but their flying range is moving north with climate change. Caterpillars (called orange dogs or orange puppies) can be a pest on citrus farms. Adults mostly inhabit deciduous forest (and citrus orchards farther south) although they can also be found in gardens.

BRUSHFOOTS (*NYMPHALIDAE*)

Brushfoots are the largest family of butterflies with over 6000 species worldwide. Brushfoots generally only use four legs, while holding the front two tightly folded against their body just below their head. Some species have stiff brush-like hairs (called setae) which contributes to their name.

The black "V" (above) are the two front legs folded against the body (I adjusted the contrast to show the legs—below is unaltered).

Brushfoot butterflies have several subfamilies and genera including: Admirals (*Limenitidinae*), Emperors (*Apaturinae*), Monarchs (*Danainae*), Fritillaries (*Heliconiinae*), Snouts (*Libytheinae*), Satyrs (*Satyrinae*), and True Brushfoots (*Nymphalinae*). Vermont has several Brushfoots that are rare or endangered (see page 53 for details).

Technically, members of the genus *Limenitis* are Admirals. That means Vermont has two Admirals: *Limenitis archippus,* the Viceroy (which looks like a Monarch) and *Limenitis arthemis,* which includes two forms once called the White Admiral and the Red-Spotted Purple, but now together called Red-Spotted Admirals.

Limenitis artemis x Limenitis archippus hybrid.

The Red Admiral sounds like it should be included with Admirals (and I have put it with them) but it is actually in the genus *Vanessa* and technically should be listed with the True Brushfoots. Fortunately, these butterflies are easy to tell apart, and otherwise, it's just the name.

We have several difficult Fritillaries in the area. First, note that the Great Spangled Fritillary is the largest. It also has the widest cream pm band on the underwing. To distinguish the smaller Atlantis and Aphrodite Fritillaries look to their eyes. The Atlantis Fritillary has blue-gray eyes while the Great Spangled and Aphrodite both have amber eyes.

Once you have studied one species you can start to notice differences in the one you know and the others. From there you can learn to see the subtle differences between species. These and other small differences will become more apparent with time and practice. Until then learning to recognize the overall form of a Fritillary can be useful.

Satyrs, including the Browns, are a medium sized species of the Family *Nymphalidae*. Don't overlook these subtle beauties simply-because they lack the eye-popping color of other butterflies. The Eyed Brown is similar to the rarely seen Appalachian Brown.

Common Wood Nymph.

Included under True Brushfoots are the Commas. You might think that a butterfly that is bright orange and black with distinctive scalloped wings would be hard to miss. Yet, with wings folded Commas and Question Marks resemble nothing so much as a dead leaf.

On Commas the underside of the wing is broken by a small white curve reminiscent of the punctuation mark which gives them their name. The Question Mark has a dot beneath the curve, turning the comma into a question mark. In Vermont the Eastern Comma is the most common. Unfortunately for identification, it also changes color over the season, with summer individuals showing more black, making Commas and Question Marks difficult to distinguish.

Eastern Comma.

Pearl and Northern Crescents are a pair of butterflies that even experts have trouble identifying. The last I heard, they were best distinguished by looking at the bottom of their antenna clubs, while a few experts consider them a single species. Because of that I recommend not bothering to distinguish them and just enjoying them as Crescents. I've listed them both under genus *Phyciodes*.

Other True Brushfoots include Checkerspots and Tortoiseshells, which tend to be relatively easy to identify. We have only one Snout in Vermont. It's a rare vagrant and I can't wait to see one. Other rare or unusual Brushfoots include the Tawny and Hackberry Emperors and the Jutta Arctic.

Baltimore Checkerspot.

— Monarch (*Danaus plexippus*) —

(XL)

Flies May–Oct

Adults feed on milkweed, but also nectar on asters, lilac, and joe pye weed.

Many people love Vermont's State Butterfly, the Monarch. While it was recently listed as threatened it is not the most endangered Vermont butterfly (see page 53). Loss of habitat, herbicides and other dangers along its migratory route all add to the risks the species is now facing. Its habitat includes any area with milkweed.

Host plants are milkweeds.

— Viceroy (*Limenitis archippus*) —

(Lg)

Flies May–Sept

Early season adults feed on aphid honeydew, dung, and carrion. Later in the season, they nectar on flowers.

The Viceroy gains protection by mimicking Monarchs who are toxic to predators. A second glance shows the difference, as Viceroys have a distinct black line across their HW that is seen with wings both open and closed. Their habitat includes wet and open areas with willows.

Host plants are willow, aspen, and poplar.

KATE TAYLOR

— Red Admiral (*Vanessa atalanta*) —

(Lg)

Flies Late April–Oct

Adults nectar on flowers, but prefer tree sap, fermenting fruit, and bird droppings.

Host plants are mainly nettles, but also hemp, hops, and hackberry.

Red Admirals are in the genus *Vanessa*. A brilliant red-orange median band on the FW blends into a wide marginal band on the HW. Underwings are mottled black-brown with red on the FW. Red Admirals migrate annually from the South. They prefer wet meadows, and open areas including fields and moist meadows near woodlands.

— Red-Spotted Admiral (*Limenitis arthemis astyanax*) —

(Lg)

Flies May–Aug

Adults feed on sap from host trees, rotting fruit, and sometimes white flowers.

Host plants are trees and shrubs such as poplar, birch, cherry, willow, and oak.

The Red-Spotted Admiral species now includes two subspecies. Those shown here used to be called Red-Spotted Purples, while the ones on page 12 were White Admirals. They are now considered a single species. Their preferred habitat is moist woodlands but they can be seen in a variety of habitats.

— Red-Spotted Admiral (*Limenitis arthemis arthemis*) —

(Lg)

Flies June–Sept

Adults feed on sap of host trees, or on rotting fruit and sometimes from white flowers.

The White Admiral is technically a Red-Spotted Admiral, the same species as shown on page 11. The white band is a recessive trait, common in Vermont. The upper-side of the white form is mostly dark blue, almost black, with white PM bands across the wings and a row of spots on the margin and just above. They like rich conifer and mixed wood openings and nearby areas.

Host plants include aspen, cherry, birch, poplar, and willow.

— Great Spangled Fritillary (*Argynnis cybele*) —

(XL)

Flies June–Oct

Adults nectar on joe pye weed, milkweed, and many others.

These large, active butterflies are common and widespread in Vermont. They are larger than other Fritillaries in our area and they have the widest cream band on their HW. They have amber eyes. They like open fields and meadows, including wet meadows where they are often seen with Atlantis Fritillaries.

Host plants are in the violet family.

— Atlantis Fritillary (*Argynnis atlantis*) —

Flies June–End Sept

Adults nectar on joe pye weed, milkweed, and many others.

Host plants are in the violet family.

Atlantis Fritillaries are often confused with Aphrodite, but note the blue-grey eyes of the Atlantis. The Great Spangled Fritillary has a wider band than the Atlantis. Atlantis Fritillaries are generally smaller than Aphrodite or Great Spangled Fritillaries. Habitat is open, mixed woodlands as well as moist meadows and wood openings.

— Aphrodite Fritillary (*Argynnis aphrodite*) —

Flies Late June–Early Sept

Adults nectar on joe pye weed, milkweed, and others.

Host plants are in the violet family.

The Aphrodite Fritillary is smaller than the Great Spangled Fritillary, and is often found in the same area. Look for amber eyes and a narrow or sometimes missing cream band on the underside of the HW. Edges of wings are lightly silvered. Its preferred habitat is moist meadows and open woods, as well as transition areas.

— Silver-Bordered Fritillary (*Boloria myrina*) —

(Med)

Flies May–Sept

Adults nectar on joe pye weed, milkweed, and many others.

Host plants are in the violet family.

The Silver-bordered Fritillary isn't particularly silver except in relation to the other fritillaries. Wing borders can be (but aren't always) silvered. The underside is more of a rusty red-orange than other Fritillaries and the white spots on the hind wings are in the margin. If you are expecting the more common Fritillaries it will stand out. It prefers bogs, wet meadows, and marshes.

— Meadow Fritillary (*Boloria bellona*) —

(Med)

Flies May–Sept

Adults nectar on joe pye weed, milkweed, and many others.

Host plants are in the violet family.

The Meadow Fritillary lacks white spots on the underwing. It also lacks a solid black margin on the upper HW. Once you recognize the others the Meadow Fritillary will "just look different." It isn't quite as bright, it's a bit smaller, and it looks unfamiliar if you have mostly seen the three common Frits. It prefers wet, grassy fields and meadows.

— Common Ringlet (*Coenonympha california*) —

Flies May–Sept

Adults nectar on blackberry, hawkweed, clover, bedstraw, and cinquefoil.

Host plants include many grasses, as well as some rushes and sedges.

Common Ringlets can be varied in shade or color tone depending on wear. They are often bright, tawny brown, sometimes bordering on orange. Other times they are closer to gray or even cream. Look for a tiny white spot, surrounded by black, circled by cream, on the FW. Common Ringlets can be abundant in grassy fields and meadows, roadsides, yards, and other open habitat.

— Common Wood-Nymph (*Cercyonis pegala*) —

(Med)

Flies June–Sept

Adults nectar on flowers as well as dung and rotting fruit.

Host plants include many grasses.

The Common Wood-Nymph has a mottled brown background that looks almost ridged with 2 large eyespots on the FW. On some individuals these eyespots are within a contrasting cream area. Other individuals have less cream or lack it altogether. The subtlety of the coloring is worth a second look. They prefer a habitat of sunny meadows, woodlands, and grassy areas.

— Eyed Brown (*Lethe eurydice*) —

(Med)

Flies May–Aug

Adults nectar on sap and bird droppings, sometimes on flowers.

Eyed Browns have a soft, tan ground color with thin, wavy, brown bands. Their forewings have four eyespots in a cream background with more on their HW. They are larger than the Little Wood Satyr and have more eyespots. The Appalachian Brown looks similar but is less common in Vermont. They like wet meadows, swamps, and marshes with sedges.

Host plants are sedges.

— Little Wood Satyr (*Megisto cymela*) —

(Med)

Flies May–Aug

Adults nectar on sap, aphid secretions, and rotting materials.

The Little Wood Satyr has fewer eyespots than the Eyed Brown and they are directly on the background, not in a pod. The HW spots tend to blend together. It is larger than the Common Ringlet and smaller than the Common Wood-Nymph or Eyed Brown. It prefers open grasslands, deep woods, and brushy fields near woods.

Host plants include grasses, particularly orchard grass and blue grass.

KATE TAYLOR

— Northern Pearly-Eye (*Lethe anthedon*) —

Flies June–Sept

Adults nectar on tree sap as well as dung and carrion.

Host plants include many grasses.

The Northern Pearly-Eye is similar in appearance to the Eyed Brown, but with larger and bolder eyespots. They tend to have a darker background color than Eyed Browns. They like low light and can be seen flying at dusk. They like shade more than many other butterflies. They prefer wet, deciduous woods and open forests, especially with a grassy understory.

— Mourning Cloak (*Nymphalis antiopa*) —

Flies March–Sept

Adults nectar on sap from various trees.

Host plants are willows, also poplars, birches, elm, and hackberry.

The Mourning Cloak overwinters and can fly as early as February. When the air is cold they shiver to raise their temperature. Their background is chocolate brown with white margins and blue spots. They prefer hardwood forests, but they may be found in many habitats including fields. When you are sick of winter, head out and look for these signs of spring.

— Painted Lady (*Vanessa cardui*) —

(Med)

Flies May–Frost

Adults nectar on thistles, clover, and milkweed, among other flowers.

The Painted Lady can't survive Vermont winters and migrates annually from southern climates. The underside of the HW is a colorful cobweb design with four or five eyespots from the sm to pm band area. Its habitat is varied and includes open sunny areas such as waste lots, gardens, fields, farmlands, and roadsides.

Host plants include members of the mallow family, lupines, and other legumes.

— American Lady (*Vanessa virginiensis*) —

(Med)

Flies April–Oct

Adults nectar on aster, dogbane, goldenrod, and others.

The American Lady has a colorful cobweb design on the underside of the wings with two large eyespots. When resting with wings open the American Lady usually has a small white dot in a cell in the pm area of the forewing. Preferred habitat is open and sunny. Both Ladies like to frequent flower gardens.

Host plants include pearly everlasting, cud weeds, pussytoes, and others.

— Eastern Comma (*Polygonia comma*) —

(Med)

Flies April–Oct

Adults nectar on rotting fruit and tree sap.

Host plants are elm, nettle, and hops.

The Eastern Comma overwinters as an adult. Spring adults tend to have orange HW with black spots while the summer form has more black. Their topside has different amounts of black depending on the individual, but there is always a distinctive white "comma" on the underside of the HW. They prefer woodlands and adjacent openings, wet meadows, and disturbed areas.

— Gray Comma (*Polygonia progne*) —

(Sm) (Med)

Flies March–Oct

Adults nectar on sap, dung, and decaying matter.

Host plants include currants and gooseberries.

The Gray Comma overwinters as an adult. Its upper wings are bright orange and brown, usually with small yellow spots in HW black border. Its summer form has a wide dark border. The "comma" on the underwing is more "L" shaped than the other commas who have more of a crescent-shaped comma. They like open areas within forests, as well as yards and roadsides.

BUTTERFLIES OF VERMONT

— Green Comma (*Polygonia faunus*) —

(Med)

Flies April–Sept

Adults nectar on flowers, dung, and carrion.

Green Commas have a dark margin on their topsides and are mottled brown underneath. In the right light the green on their underside is obvious and they have the comma of their name. They have ragged wings. They overwinter as adults and are seen throughout the flying season. Their habitat is stream sides, openings in hardwood, or mixed woodlands and dirt roads.

Host plants include willows, birches, and alders.

— Question Mark (*Polygonia interrogationis*) —

(Lg)

Flies June–Oct

Adults nectar on rotting fruit, dung, carrion, and rarely on flowers.

Question Marks are larger than commas and have a hooked forewing. They have a zigzagging flight that often returns them to their starting point. You will learn this as you run after them only to run back the way you came. They like woodlands and adjacent openings, as well as open spaces.

Host plants are hackberries, nettles, and plants in the elm family.

— Baltimore Checkerspot (*Euphydryas phaeton*) —

(Med)

Flies June–Aug

Adults nectar on a large number of flowers.

Host plants include members of the figwort family, especially turtlehead and plantains.

The Baltimore Checkerspot is beautifully decorated with orange and white on a black background. Its bright coloring cannot be mistaken for any other Vermont butterfly. When in doubt just admire the striking orange clubs on the end of the antennas. They tend to prefer marshes/wet meadows but they can also be found in dry fields.

— Harris' Checkerspot (*Chlosyne harrisii*) —

(Med)

Flies June–Aug

Adults nectar on many different flowers.

Host plants are flat-topped asters.

Harris' Checkerspots are orange and black above with additional white below. Folded wings show a geometric design including squares, rectangles, and chevrons. Male Harrises like to puddle and can be seen nectaring on minerals in wet areas. They tend to be found near their host plants. Their preferred habitat is wet meadows, and marsh borders with their host plants.

— Pearl and Northern Crescents (*Phyciodes sp.*) —

(Sm)

Flies May–Sept

Adults nectar on a wide variety of plants.

Pearl and Northern Crescents are butterflies that even the experts find hard to distinguish. The sexes are different and characteristics of one species overlap with the other. I recommend not trying to id the species and just enjoy them as Crescents. They like to perch on flowers with wings open, enjoying the sun. They like open areas such as fields and disturbed areas.

Host plants are asters.

— Compton Tortoiseshell (*Nymphalis l-album*) —

(Lg) (XL)

Flies late June and fall

Adults nectar on sap, rotting fruit, dung, and occasionally and willow.

Compton Tortoiseshells overwinter as adults, flying in early spring. They can live for 10 months, making them one of Vermont's longest-lived butterflies. Their lower HW includes a white slash similar to that of Commas, although more of a backward L shape. They prefer a forest habitat, especially moist areas.

Host plants include aspen, willows, gray birch, and paper birch.

— Milbert's Tortoiseshell (*Aglais milberti*) —

(Med)

Flies March–Oct

Adults nectar on a wide variety of plants.

Host plants are nettles.

Milbert's Tortoiseshell has a wide orange sm band across both HW and FW, with a thin band of blue spots in the sm on the topside of its wings. Its bright topside contrasts with a chocolate-brown underwing that shows a light band as if the orange was fading through from the top. Their preferred habitat is open fields, usually moist, near woodlands or streams, and weedy meadows.

QUIZ: WHICH IS NOT A BRUSHFOOT?

From left: Monarch, Gray Squirrel, American Lady.

GOSSAMERWINGS (*LYCAENIDAE*)

Gossamerwings are a family of butterflies, usually on the smaller side, who typically perch with wings folded. They get their name because many of them have brightly colored upper wings. There are four major sub-families: Coppers (*Lycaeninae*), Harvesters (*Miletinae*), Blues (*Polyommatinae*), and Elfins and Hairstreaks (*Theclinae*).

Azure.

We have three Coppers in Vermont, the American Copper (*Lycaena phlaeas*), the Bronze Copper (*Lycaena hyllus*), and the Bog Copper (*Lycaena epixanthe*). The Bog Copper is rare and confined to cranberry bogs. It is one of the smallest Vermont butterflies, and is hard to see, even if you are on top of it.

Blues and Azures get their name from their blue upper wings. The color ranges from sapphire to gray-blue depending on species and sex. Most often you will see these small butterflies resting with wings together. They are easy to overlook, but some of my favorite butterflying time has been spent admiring these tiny insects.

Azure in flight.

The Spring Azure, once a perfectly respectable species, is presently in a state of confusion as more research is breaking the species into several different ones (up to six, but more often three species). Experts agree that they are "difficult" to tell apart. When someone who studies butterflies for a living says "difficult," I say, better to call it an Azure, and leave the details to others.

Fortunately, these small beauties don't care what you call them. You may first notice them as stray motes of blue fluttering past. Pay attention to where they land, because when they fold their wings they can become invisible.

In Vermont the Elfin you are most likely to see is the Eastern Pine Elfin (*Callophrys niphon*). Vermont has a few other uncommon or rare Elfins, including the elusive Bog Elfin (*Callophrys lanoraieensis*). Of this creature Jeffrey Glassberg says: "If you are willing to travel to remote Black Spruce bogs and feed ravenous mosquitoes and black flies, you'll have a chance of missing this mysterious butterfly yet again" (*Swift Guide to Butterflies*).

The Bog Elfin is so rare in Vermont that it wasn't until 2023 that Bryan Pfeiffer confirmed that this wonderful creature makes its home here in Vermont.

At first glance Elfins are small, drab creatures. A second glance may confirm that impression. But they are worth the effort. The Eastern Pine Elfin is an elegant beauty, and a common sight as well. While it may seem dull a closer look shows an array of colors that bring delight to the beholder.

Brown Elfin.

Elfins are among the earliest fliers of the butterfly season, so look for them in the spring. Look carefully. It is easy to look right past them, as they tend to blend in with their surroundings.

Hairstreaks are another subfamily of the Gossamerwings. Vermont has many Hairstreaks, but most are rarely seen. The Banded Hairstreak (*Satyrium calanus*) is the most common, but the Coral Hairstreak (*Satyrium titus*) and the Striped Hairstreak (*Satyrium liparops*) are also quite common. Hairstreaks are elusive creatures and I'm always happy to see one.

Coral Hairstreak.

BUTTERFLIES OF VERMONT

— American Copper (*Lycaena hypophlaeas*) —

(Sm)

Flies April–Oct

Adults nectar on a variety of flowers, including clover and buttercup.

Host plants include dock and sheep sorrel.

American Coppers are small, with intense orange to red wings, elongated black spots on top, and orange and gray/white underwings with black spots. When wings are folded they can be distinguished from the Bronze Copper by the narrow, jagged, orange line on their HM margin. They prefer disturbed open areas, but they are also found in fields and grasslands.

— Bronze Copper (*Lycaena hyllus*) —

(Med)

Flies June–Sept

Adults nectar on blackberry and clover.

Host plants include docks, especially water dock.

Bronze Coppers are larger than American Coppers. Females range from orange to yellow. Males are darker, copper brown. The orange band on their HW is wider than on the American Copper. Their habitat includes wet meadows and marshes, especially river flood plains.

— Azure (*Celastrina sp.*) —

(Sm)

Flies April–Sept

Adults nectar on vetch, yarrow, meadowsweet, cinquefoil, and others.

Host plants include dogwood, New Jersey tea, and meadowsweet.

These butterflies are pale gray to dusty brown below. Mid-summer Azures tend to be light. They can have dark margins on the lower wings along with spots and lines of brown. The top wing is bright blue in the males and darker in the females. They prefer perching with wings closed. They like partially open areas and transition zones, particularly stream banks and forest edges.

— Eastern Tailed Blue (*Cupido comyntas*) —

(Tiny)

Flies May–Oct

Adults nectar on clover as well as aster and cinquefoil.

Host plants include clover and alfalfa.

This is the smallest Vermont blue and it is particularly eye-catching. The underside of its wings are pale gray, dotted with black. The HW has three large, orange spots that look like chevrons. Look for the tiny "tails" on the HW near the orange spots. They like open areas including disturbed areas. They come to the area of my lawn that I have left wild.

BUTTERFLIES OF VERMONT

— Silvery Blue (*Glaucopsyche lygdamus*) —

(Sm)

Flies in springtime.

Adults nectar on many flowers including strawberry, fleabane, vetch, and dogwood.

These butterflies are similar to the Spring Azure, with a background color that is blue-gray. But, where the Spring Azure's markings can seem haphazard, the Silvery Blue is marked with bold, black spots and lines surrounded by white/cream. They like open and damp woods, meadows, roadsides, brushy areas, bogs, and other open habitats.

Host plants are vetch, peavine, and other legumes.

— Eastern Pine Elfin (*Callophrys niphon*) —

(Sm)

Flies April–July

Adults nectar on blueberry, cinquefoil, and milkweed.

Host plants include pines.

At first these small butterflies seem like a drab brown, but if you look closely you can see colors, ranging from silver to maroon to deep purple. They are delightful creatures that like to rub their wings together as they sit to be admired. Look for them early in spring. They prefer pine forests and deciduous woodland mixed with pines.

— Banded Hairstreak (*Satyrium calanus*) —

Flies June–Aug
Adults nectar at a variety of flowers including dogbane, milkweed, and New Jersey tea.

Host plants include oak, walnut, and hickory.

The Banded Hairstreak has a gray-brown background color with wavy stripes and lines of darker brown, frosted with white. It has two sets of tails with longer ones on the bottom, although they are often missing. Near the tails is a sporty, blue area with orange spots above. They prefer mixed forests and edges and nearby open areas.

— Coral Hairstreak (*Satyrium titus*) —

Flies June–Aug

Adults nectar on milkweed, dogbane, and New Jersey tea.

Host plants are cherry and plum.

This is the only Vermont Hairstreak without tails. The underside of the hindwing is light brown with a row of bright coral spots at the margin, and a pm row of black spots rimmed with white. As an added bonus, the tips of their antenna clubs are coral. They prefer weedy habitats near food sources, brushy fields, overgrown orchards, and roads.

— Striped Hairstreak *(Satyrium liparops)* —

(Sm)

Flies June–Aug

Adults nectar from milkweed, dogbane, goldenrod, and New Jersey tea.

The Striped Hairstreak is similar to the Banded Hairstreak except it is more gray than brown and the blue spot is capped with a bright orange chevron. It has two tails on its HW. Like other Hairstreaks these are small butterflies that require a good eye to spot. They like deciduous forest openings and edges, stream sides, and shaded swamps.

Host plants include cherries, blueberries, and other shrubs.

— Harvester *(Feniseca tarquinius)* —

(Sm)

Flies May–Aug

Adults nectar on sap, scat, and aphid honeydew.

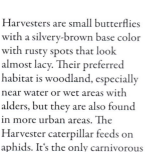

Harvesters are small butterflies with a silvery-brown base color with rusty spots that look almost lacy. Their preferred habitat is woodland, especially near water or wet areas with alders, but they are also found in more urban areas. The Harvester caterpillar feeds on aphids. It's the only carnivorous caterpillar in North America.

Host plants are those with Woolly Aphids, especially alder or beech.

WHITES AND YELLOWS (*PIERIDAE*)

Whites and Yellows are the common, pale butterflies that are so often seen flying around fields. They may seem dull compared to brightly colored Swallowtails or flamboyant Gossamerwings, but take a closer look. Depending on the species you will see delicate pink wing edges, large green eyes, or orange spots. Some species have soaring flights that take them across a meadow and back, leaving you nothing to do but admire them.

Clouded Sulphur.

Vermont has two subfamilies, the Sulphurs (*Coliadinae*) and the Whites (*Pierinae*). The common Sulphurs are the Orange Sulphur (*Colias eurytheme*) and the Clouded Sulphur (*Colias philodice*). The Pink-Edged Sulphur (*Colias interior*) is seen occasionally.

Mustard Whites.

Whites include the ubiquitous Cabbage White (*Pieris rapae*), which is easy to raise from a caterpillar. If you have a garden, don't kill those little green larvae on your cabbage; bring one in and raise it to adult (feeding it on said cabbage) then set it free and watch it fly.

The Mustard White (*Pieris oleracea*) is also common and looks similar to the West Virginia White (*Pieris virginiensis*), which is seen occasionally in Vermont woods.

Cabbage White chrysalis (above), caterpillar (center), and adult (bottom).

— Orange Sulphur (*Colias eurytheme*) —

(Med)

Flies May–Nov

Adults nectar on flowers including dandelion, milkweed, and goldenrod.

The Orange Sulphur and the Clouded Sulphur can be difficult to identify. However, the sexes are easy, so you can still impress your friends. Males are yellow, while females can be yellow, white, off white, or have a greenish tinge. They have yellow or white spots in the black wing margin, while males have pure black margins. They prefer open habitat, especially meadows.

Host plants are legumes such as clover and alfalfa.

— Clouded Sulphur (*Colias philodice*) —

(Med)

Flies April–Oct

Adults nectar on flowers including dandelion, milkweed, and goldenrod.

Clouded Sulphurs are common in fields. They have yellow upper wings with solid black spots. The underside of the hindwing has a spot rimmed with orange or pink, often doubled. Females can be white, off white, or green-white. Males' upper wings have a solid black margin, while the females have spots in the margin. Their preferred habitat is open fields.

Host plants are legumes such as clover and alfalfa.

— Mustard White (*Pieris oleracea*) —

(Med)

Flies April–Aug

Adults nectar on plants in the mustard family.

Host plants are mustards.

The Mustard White is a plain, white butterfly with strongly marked veins, especially in the summer. They have a distinctive yellow spot on their "shoulder" where the HW joins the thorax. They prefer northern deciduous forests. Because of Mustard Whites you can't glance at any white butterfly and assume it's a Cabbage White (although by the numbers, it probably is).

— Cabbage White (*Pieris rapae*) —

(Med)

Flies April–Oct

Adults nectar on mustards, dandelion, clover, aster, mint, and more.

Host plants are mustards including cabbage, broccoli, and others.

The Cabbage White is almost entirely white although it can have a yellowish hue on the underside of its wings. The upper sides have one (male) or two (female) black or gray spots and similarly colored patches of gray or black on the apex of the FW. In the spring they tend to be lighter in color. Habitats include open areas, gardens, roadsides, and agricultural fields.

SKIPPERS (*HESPERIIDAE*)

Skippers are a large family of butterflies. Vermont has around 40 species including many that are endangered and some that are critically endangered (see page 53). The more we are able to conserve their habitat the better their chances of survival. While you are unlikely to see some of the most endangered Skippers, you can still find the more common species of these miniature wonders during your travels.

Grass Skipper.

Overall, Skippers are small and often chunky with large eyes in relation to their bodies. They are strong fliers because of their muscular bodies, but they generally don't travel far. They have bent clubs on the ends of their antenna, which gives them a rakish look. Many people ignore them, but I adore them.

Identifying Skippers can be difficult. Begin by trying to place the tiny beauty into its group. In Vermont we have mostly Spreadwing Skippers (Subfamily: *Pyrginae*), and Grass Skippers (Subfamily: *Hesperiinae*) which includes two Roadside Skippers and one Skipperling. While you may not be able to identify species, it is relatively easy to decide which of these groups it belongs to.

Spreadwing Skipper.

The Spreadwing Skippers, as their name suggests, usually perch with their wings spread. They are larger than other Skippers and often have mottled or frosty topwings. They include the Cloudywing Skippers and the Silver-Spotted Skipper. The Silver-Spotted Skipper, despite belonging to the Spreadwings, usually nectars with wings closed. It is the easiest of the Skippers to identify, due to its large silver spot.

Grass Skipper.

Vermont has many Grass Skippers and they are hard to distinguish. They often vary in their posture, including resting with hindwings spread and forewings raised to form a "V" shape. To make them more confusing, the sexes can have different amounts or strength of spotting, the time of year can fade the color of individuals, and the way the wings are held can hide markings. Together that can make it hard to determine species unequivocally, but it's worth a try and they won't care if you get it wrong.

— Pepper and Salt Skipper (*Amblyscirtes hegon*) —

 Tiny

Flies May–July

Adults nectar from viburnum and blackberry, among others.

Host plants include grasses such as bluegrass and Indian grass.

Pepper and Salt Skippers are tiny with an underwing ground color that is mostly gray with a green tinge to it. The overall coloration is frosted rather than solid, although there is a white pm band on both the HW and FW which lacks the mottled look of the rest of the wing. Their habitat includes open woods and edges, especially near streams in glades.

— Common Roadside Skipper (*Amblyscirtes vialis*) —

Tiny

Flies June–July

Adults nectar from low growing blue flowers like selfheal and verbena.

Host plants are various grasses.

The Common Roadside Skipper is similar to the Pepper and Salt Skipper (above) but has a darker background color with less frosting. It often lacks the white PM band on the HW. They often search for minerals in damp, bare earth. They live in various habitats, preferring open areas near woodlands and streams.

— Arctic Skipper (*Carterocephalus mandan*) —

(Sm)

Flies May–July

Adults nectar on geranium, as well as blackberry and iris.

The Arctic Skipper is Vermont's only Skipperling. Its wings are strongly patterned. The upper wings are dark with geometric orange spots. The underside is red-orange with cream to whitish spots outlined in dark brown-black. Its habitat is moist, grassy, open areas within or adjacent to oak-pine transition forest.

Host plants are grasses.

— Peck's Skipper (*Polites peckius*) —

(Sm)

Flies end May–Sept

Adults nectar from milkweed, dogbane, clover, and others.

Peck's Skipper is orange-brown with orange-cream basal and pm bands. The middle portion of the pm band is wider than the rest of the band. When perched with wings spread it has many orange to cream spots on either an orange-brown or a brown-orange background. They are grass skippers and like grassy habitats such as meadows, gardens, fields, and roadsides.

Host plants are various grasses.

— Hobomok Skipper (*Lon hobomok*) —

Flies May–July

Adults nectar on milkweed, dogbane, clover, and blackberry.

Host plants are grasses.

Hobomok Skippers are Grass Skippers similar to Peck's, often with a darker background color. The orange-cream area can be a single sloppy spot, rather than distinct bands. The edges of their underwings are frosty. Females have a dark, purple-black form as well. They prefer woodland habitats and are often seen in clearings or openings and edges, especially in damp areas.

— Long Dash (*Polites mystic*) —

Sm

Flies May–Aug

Adults will nectar on most flowering plants in their habitat.

Host plants are blue grasses.

Long Dash Skippers have wide, bold spotting on the HW. They are orange-brown with strong markings similar to Peck's and Hobomok Skippers. They are Grass Skippers and they live in many different habitats, especially open, wet, grassy areas.

— Sassacus Skipper (*Hesperia sassacus*) —

(Sm)

Flies May–July

Adults nectar on flowers such as blackberry and phlox.

Previously known as Indian Skippers, the Sassacus Skipper looks like the Long Dash, but is usually a bit paler. They are Grass Skippers and like other Skippers can be hard to see. Look for a flash of orange-brown among the grass. Their favored habitats are old fields and grasslands.

Host plants are various grasses including Little Bluestem and panic grasses.

— Leonard's Skipper (*Hesperia leonardus*) —

(Sm)

Flies Mid Aug–Mid Sept

Adults nectar on thistle and aster, but prefer Blazing Star.

Leonard's Skipper is a Grass Skipper that tends to be more reddish-orange than the others. It has a strong pattern of spots on its underside. Populations may be declining in the east. Look for them a bit later in the season, starting in August. Their habitat is variable, but they tend to favor open grassy areas.

Host plants are various perennial grasses.

— Dun Skipper (*Euphyes vestris*) —

Flies June–Aug

Adults nectar on a variety of white, pink, or purple flowers.

Host plants are sedges.

The Dun Skipper is a small Grass Skipper with light-brown to dark yellow-orange wings. The underside of the wings are faintly patterned with cloudy spots. Their preferred habitat is moist, open areas, and woodland clearings and edges.

— Little Glassywing (*Vernia verna*) —

Flies June–Sept

Adults nectar predominantly on milkweed.

Host plants are grasses, including purpletop grasses.

Little Glassywings have darker wings than some of the other Grass Skippers. Their underside often has a reddish hue, although it is not as deep an orange as Leonard's Skipper. They prefer wet fields near woods, but are also found in drier habitats.

— Northern Broken-Dash (*Polites egeremet*) —

(Sm)

Flies June–Sept

Adults favor white, pink, or purple flowers such as clover, milkweed, and dogbane.

The Northern Broken-Dash is similar to both Little Glassywings and Dun Skippers. The bottom of the HW shows a curve of spots with a faint center spot pointing inward. One of the Grass Skippers, their preferred habitat includes grassy fields and meadows, including disturbed areas.

Host plants are grasses, especially panic grass.

— Tawny-Edged Skipper (*Polites themistocles*) —

(Sm)

Flies May–Sept

Adults nectar on a number of flowers including clover, vetch, thistle, and dogbane.

At first glance this Grass Skipper has no markings on its topside, but when its wings are together the top of the FW shows brighter orange, giving the wings a tawny look. Their habitat includes a range of grassy, open areas including damp meadows, prairie swales, lawns, and vacant lots.

Host plants are grasses, including panic grass, bluegrass, and crabgrass.

— Least Skipper (*Ancyloxypha numitor*) —

(Tiny)

Flies May–Sept

Adults nectar from low growing plants such as sorrel, verbena, and clover.

Host plants include grasses, especially bluegrass and rice nutgrass.

A white thorax and short antennas help identify this Grass Skipper. As its name suggests, it is one of the smallest Skippers. A quick scan of a field will usually miss them. They like wet grassy areas including marshes, meadows, and roadside ditches.

— Delaware Skipper (*Anatrytone logan*) —

(Sm)

Flies June–Aug

Adults nectar on pink and white flowers including milkweed, mint, thistle, and others.

Host plants are grasses and sedges.

Delaware Skippers are Grass Skippers with bright orange-yellow wings. The undersides are plain with no markings. The upper sides have dark borders. Their preferred habitats are open, brushy fields, moist meadows, and sedge marshes.

— European Skipper (*Thymelicus lineola*) —

(Sm)

Flies June–July

Adults nectar from low growing flowers and prefer hawkweed, thistle, milkweed, and others.

European Skippers are an introduced species that are starting to outnumber all other Vermont Skippers during their flying period. One of the Grass Skippers, they prefer open, grassy meadows, especially with tall grasses, abandoned homesteads, damp fields, road edges and even gardens.

Host plants are grasses, mainly timothy.

— Silver-Spotted Skipper (*Epargyreus clarus*) —

(Med)

Flies May–Sept

Adults almost never visit yellow flowers, preferring clover, thistle, vetch, and milkweed.

The Silver-Spotted Skipper is large (for a Skipper) and easy to identify; just look for the large silver (white) spot. Its wings are brown-black with an orange band on the FW visible with wings open and closed. Their preferred habitat is woodland borders and openings, but they are also found in meadows, especially with vetch.

Host plants include vetch, locust, trefoil, and other legumes.

KATE TAYLOR

— Wild Indigo Duskywing (*Erynnis babtisae*) —

Flies May–Sept

Adults nectar on blackberry, dogbane, New Jersey tea, and lupine.

Host plants include lupine, vetch, and of course, wild indigo.

The Wild Indigo Duskywing is a Spreadwing Skipper. It is slightly smaller than other Duskywings. It looks similar to the rare Columbine and Persius Duskywings. It has a range of habitats, preferring open areas such as fields and meadows, but also including places with poor soil. Its population is increasing in Vermont.

— Northern Cloudywing (*Thorybes pylades*) —

Med

Flies May–July

Adults nectar on dogbane, vetch, thistle and others.

Host plants include those in the legume (pea) family.

One of the Spreadwing Skippers. The upper side is dark brown with clear, unaligned spots on the forewing. The underside is mottled with lighter edges. The Northern Cloudywing doesn't have much patterning compared with other Spreadwings. It likes dry, open habitat, including fields and roadsides.

— Dreamy Duskywing (*Erynnis icelus*) —

(Sm)

Flies May–July

Adults nectar on blueberry, dogbane, New Jersey tea, and lupine.

The Dreamy Duskywing is a Spreadwing Skipper with forewings that are more heavily frosted than other Duskywings. Dreamy Duskywings are generalists and can be found in a variety of open habitats such as woodland openings and edges, stream sides, and fields.

Host plants include willow, aspen, and birch.

— Juvenal's Duskywing (*Erynnis juvenalis*) —

(Med)

Flies May–July

Adults nectar on dandelion, cherry, wisteria, and others.

Juvenal's Duskywings are another Spreadwing Skipper. Female Juvenal's tend to have a lighter brown base color than the males. Both sexes have triangular white spots in their top forewings. Juvenal's Duskywings like many habitats including oak woods, edges and trails, and scrub oak barrens.

Host plants include various oaks.

HOST PLANTS

What follows are a few examples of plants that butterflies use as host plants to lay their eggs on and that caterpillars feed on. Please note that this list is in no way complete; it is meant as a starting point for further exploration.

Eastern Comma

Why focus on caterpillar host plants? It's simple: without caterpillars there are no butterflies, so focusing on their food source is a first step. For example, Monarch caterpillars will only feed on milkweed so if there is no milkweed available they cannot survive even though the adults nectar on many different flowers. Also, female butterflies will search out their host plants to lay their eggs, so you are likely to find adult butterflies if you know which host plants to look for.

American Lady

For those who like gardening, once you know the host plants you can start to add them to your garden and benefit from both new plants and new butterflies. Highly recommended!

Note: The science on host plants is still young and the information that is available today might change tomorrow as new studies are done. If you log your observations on *inaturalist, ebutterfly,* or a similar site, your data could help clarify butterfly or plant science.

As with butterflies, scientists are continually studying plants and that can cause changes in the taxonomy. None of that affects the butterflies or their plants, of course, but it makes it harder for enthusiasts to keep up. In these pages I've done my best to use the most recent science. Think of this section less as the definitive word on host plants, and more as an invitation to think about plants as they relate to butterflies.

Top to bottom: Cabbage White, Baltimore Checkerspot, White Admiral, Canadian Tiger Swallowtail

Aster Family (*Asteraceae*): pearly everlasting, pussytoes, cottonweed, sunflower, flat-topped aster ...
Hosts for Painted Lady, American Lady, Crescents

Flat Topped Asters *(Doellingeria umbellata)* — Pearly Everlasting *(Anaphalis margaritacea)* — Pussytoes *(Antennaria)* — Common Burdock *(Arctium minus)*

Beech Family (*Fagaceae*): beech, oak, chestnut ... Hosts for Banded Hairstreak, Juvenal's Duskywing, Red-Spotted Admiral, Harvester

Oak *(Quercus)* — Red Oak *(Quercus rubra)* — American Beech *(Fagus grandifolia)* — American Beech *(Fagus grandifolia)*

Birch Family (*Betulaceae*): alder, birch, American hornbeam, hazelnut... Hosts for Canadian Tiger Swallowtail, Green Comma, Compton Tortoiseshell, Dreamy Duskywing, Harvester, Red-spotted Admiral, White Admiral, Mourning Cloak, Harvester

Paper Birch *(Betula papyrifera)* — American Hazelnut *(Corylus avellana)* — Am. Hophornbeam *(Ostrya virginiana)* — Paper Birch *(Betula papyrifera)*

Buckwheat Family (*Polygonaceae*): knotweed, rhubarb, dock, sorrel...
Hosts for American Copper, Bronze Copper

Dock *(Rumex)* — Dock *(Rumex)* — Smartweed *(Persicaria)* — Wood sorrel *(Oxalis montana)*

Dogbane Family (*Apocynaceae*): milkweed, dogbane, periwinkle...
Hosts for Monarch

Swamp Milkweed   Hemp Dogbane   Common Milkweed   Common Milkweed
(*Asclepias incarnata*) (*Apocynum cannabinum*) (*Asclepias syriaca*)   (*Asclepias syriaca*)

Elm Family (*Ulmaceae*): (once included hackberry which is now in Hemp family), elm... Hosts for Eastern
Comma, Question Mark, Mourning Cloak

Elm   Slippery Elm   American Elm   Elm
(*Ulmus*)   (*Ulmus rubra*)   (*Ulmus americana*) (*Ulmus*)

Figwort Family (*Scrophulariaceae*): figwort, mullein, turtlehead ...
Hosts for Baltimore Checkerspot

Figworts   Mullein   White Turtlehead   White Turtlehead
(*Scrophularia*) (*Verbascum*)   (*Chelone glabra*)   (*Chelone glabra*)

Gooseberry Family (*Grossulariaceae*): currants, gooseberries ...
Hosts for Gray Comma

Northern Red-currant   Gooseberries and Currants   Northern Red-currant   Prickly Gooseberry
(*Ribes triste*)   (*Ribes*)   (*Ribes triste*)   (*Ribes cynosbati*)

Grass Family (*Poaceae*): orchard grass, beard grass, bluegrass, bluestem, timothy... Hosts for Common Ringlet, Common Wood-Nymph, Little Wood Satyr, Northern Pearly-Eye, Grass Skippers

Kentucky Bluegrass
(*Poa pratensis*)

Foxtails & Bristlegrass
(*Setaria viridis*)

Timothy
(*Phleum pratense*)

Big Bluestem
(*Andropogon gerardii*)

Heath Family (*Ericaceae*): rhododendron, blueberry, cranberry, labrador tea... Hosts for Striped Hairstreak, Azures

Eastern Teaberry
(*Gaultheria procumbens*)

Blueberry (*Vaccinium sect. Cyanococcus*)

Leatherleaf
(*Chamaedaphne calculate*)

Labrador Tea
(*Rhododendron groenlandicum*)

Hemp Family (*Cannabaceae*): hackberry, hemp, hops, cannabis... Hosts for Red Admiral, Mourning Cloak, Eastern Comma, Question Mark

Hackberry
(*Celtis*)

Common Hops
(*Humulus lupulus*)

Common Hackberry
(*Celtis occidentalis*)

Cannabis
(*Cannabis sativa L*)

Mallow Family (*Malvaceae*): hollyhock, musk mallow, marsh mallow... Hosts for Painted Lady

Musk Mallow
(*Malva moschata*)

Marsh Mallow
(*Althaea officinalis*)

Mallow
(*Althaea*)

Marsh Mallow
(*Althaea officinalis*)

Mustard Family (*Brassicaceae*): mustard, cabbage, broccoli, crucifers...
Hosts for Mustard White, Cabbage White

Tower Mustard (*Arabis glabra*)   Wintercress (*Barbarea vulgaris*)   Two-leaved Toothwort (*Cardamine diphylla*)   Black Mustard (*Brassica nigra*)

Nettle Family (*Urticaceae*): nettles...
Hosts for Red Admiral, Eastern Comma, Question Mark, Milbert's Tortoiseshell

Woodnettle (*Urtica*)   Great Stinging Nettle (*Urtica dioica*)   Nettles (*Utrica*)   Great Stinging Nettle (*Urtica dioica*)

Parsley Family (*Apiaceae or Umbelliferae*): carrot, queen anne's lace, dill...
Hosts for Black Swallowtail

Golden Alexander (*Zizia aurea*)   Golden Alexander (*Zizia aurea*)   Queen Anne's Lace (*Daucus carota*)   Dill (*Anethum graveolens*)

Pea Family (*Leguminosae*): alfalfa, clover, trefoil, garden peas, wild indigo, cowslips... Hosts for Eastern Tailed Blue, Silvery Blue, Orange Sulphur, Clouded Sulphur, Silver-Spotted Skipper, Northern Cloudywing, Painted Lady

Wild Lupine (*Lupinus perennis*)   Bird's-foot Trefoil (*Lotus corniculatus*)   White Clover (*Trifolium repens*)   Cow (Bird) Vetch (*Vicia cracca*)

Pine (*Pinaceae*): fir, spruce, pines, douglas fir, hemlock…
Hosts for Eastern Pine Elfin

Cedar /Arborvitae Spruce White Pine Fir
(*Cedrus*) (*Picea*) (*Pinus strobus*) (*Abies*)

Plantain Family (*Plantaginaceae*): plantain, snapdragon, speedwell …
Hosts for Baltimore Checkerspot

Speedwell Speedwell Toadflax Greater Plantain
(*Veronica*) (*Veronica*) (*Linaria vulgaris*) (*Plantago major*)

Rose Family (*Rosaceae*): plums, cherries, chokecherries, apricots, apple, peaches… Host for Question Mark, Coral Hairstreak, Striped Hairstreak, Canadian Tiger Swallowtail, Red-Spotted Purple Admiral, White Admiral, Azures

Steeplebush Cinquefoil Apple Ninebark
(*Spiraea tomentosa*) (*Potentilla*) (*Malus domestica*) (*Physocarpus*)

Rushes Family (*Juncaceae*): common rush, soft rush, somewhat-tailed rush …
Hosts to Common Ringlet

Rushes Thread Rush Flowering-Rush Bullrushes
(*Genus Juncus*) (*Juncus filiformis*) (*Butomus umbellatus*) (*Scirpoides holoschoenus*)

Sedge Family (*Cyperaceae*): true sedges, flatsedges, hop sedge... Host for Eyed Brown, Dun Skipper, Delaware Skipper, Common Ringlet

Bladder Sedge (*Carex intumescens*) Plantainleaf Sedge (*Carex plantaginea*) Flatsedges (*Genus Cyperus*) Cottongrass (*Eriophorum angustifolium*)

Violet Family (*Violaceae*): violet, pansy, johnny jump-up...Hosts for Great Spangled Fritillary, Aphrodite Fritillary, Atlantis Fritillary, Silver-Bordered Fritillary, Meadow Fritillary

Canadian Violet (*Viola canadrnsis*) Pansy (*Viola tricolor var. hortensis*) Violet (*Viola*) Sweet White Violet (*Viola blanda*)

Walnut Family (*Juglandaceae*): hickory, walnut, locust... Hosts to Banded Hairstreak

Shagbark Hickory (*Carya ovata*) Shagbark Hickory (*Carya ovata*) Eastern Black Walnut (*Juglans nigra*) Butternut (*Juglans cinerea*)

Willow Family (*Salicaceae*): willows, aspens, cottonwoods, poplar... Hosts for Viceroy, Mourning Cloak, Green Comma, Compton Tortoiseshell, Dreamy Duskywing, Red-Spotted Purple Admiral, White Admiral, Mourning Cloak, Canadian Tiger Swallowtail

Heart-leaved Willow (*Salix eriocephala*) Heart-leaved Willow (*Salix eriocephala*) Quaking Aspen (*Populus tremuloides*) Eastern Cottonwood (*Populus deltoides*)

MAKING A DIFFERENCE

Help Protect Butterflies by Protecting Their Host Plants

- Leave all, or a portion, of your lawn wild.

- Don't use pesticides or generalized weed killers.

- Remove invasive plants that crowd out butterfly-friendly plants.

- Cultivate native plants for caterpillars as well as for adult butterflies.

- Learn to recognize and encourage beneficial caterpillars.

- Redefine, or learn to love, "weeds."

- If you raise caterpillars, do it sparingly and only release adult butterflies that are already local to your area and only individuals that are disease free.

- Don't partake in mass "butterfly releases." These large releases can spread disease.

- Encourage and teach others to enjoy butterflies and other insects.

Build Awareness of Rare and Endangered Species

Vermont has many butterfly species that are rare or endangered in the state. These are listed on the facing page using information from *The Vermont Butterfly Survey 2002-2007*.

Abbreviations:
- **SX**: Extirpated in the state.
- **SGCN:** Species of Greatest Conservation Need, vulnerable to extirpation.
- **S1:** Extremely rare and of conservation concern; may be vulnerable to
- extirpation.
- **S2:** Very rare and of conservation concern; may be susceptible to extirpation.
- **S3:** Not yet susceptible to becoming extirpated in the state but may be if additional populations are destroyed.
- **S4 & S5** are not endangered.
- **SU**: Species Unrankable (due to lack of data).

For the most currant information on Vermont butterflies visit the Vermont Butterfly Atlas: ***https://val.vtecostudies.org/projects/vermont-butterfly-atlas/***

For global information visit the ICUN Red List: ***https://www.iucnredlist.org/***

Rare and Endangered Butterflies

Regal Fritillary:	**SX**	Common Sootywing	**S1**
(last observed in 1941)		Appalachian Brown	**S1S2**
Edwards' Hairstreak	**SGCN**	Silvery Checkerspot	**S1S2**
Mulberry Wing	**SGCN**	Gray Hairstreak	**S2S3**
Two-Spotted Skipper	**SGCN**	Broad-Winged Skipper	**S2S3**
Black Dash	**SGCN**	Juniper Hairstreak	**S3**
Dion Skipper	**SGCN**	Pink-Edged Sulphur	**S3**
Cobweb Skipper	**SGCN**	Hickory Hairstreak	**S3**
Dusted Skipper	**SGCN**	Brown Elfin	**S3**
Early Hairstreak	**SGCN**	Crossline Skipper	**S3**
Bog Copper	**SGCN**	Wild Indigo Duskywing	**SU**
Jutta Arctic	**SGCN**	Common Buckeye	**SU**
Hackberry Emperor	**SGCN**	Horace's Duskywing	**SU**
Tawny Emperor	**SGCN**	Henry's Elfin	**SU**
Eastern Tiger Swallowtail	**S1**	Common Checkered Skipper	**SU**
Spicebush Swallowtail	**S1**	Southern Cloudywing	**SU**
Frosted Elfin	**S1**		

These butterflies need our help. Loss of habitat, loss of biodiversity, pesticides, herbicides, and climate change are among the dangers they face. Happily, there are many ways you can make a difference. For instance, by:

Volunteering:
- for the Vermont Butterfly Atlas or other citizen science initiatives
- to help rid your neighborhood of invasive species
- to assist in passing laws to save habitat

Buying:
- organic food
- insect-friendly garden plants
- low carbon-footprint products
- only what is necessary

Talking:
- to elected officials
- to and teaching a child to love butterflies
- to and asking a neighbor to leave part of their lawn wild

Donating:
- time and/or money to research or conservation efforts

While you're at it, make your own habitat
a welcoming place for butterflies.

AT A GLANCE

The following pages list a single host plant for each Vermont butterfly. These are not the only, or even necessarily the favorite, plant for any one butterfly, but they will give you a starting point. Often a butterfly will nectar from different plants within the same plant family.

Note:
- Species marked with a red dot are of greatest concern in Vermont
- Species marked with a blue dot are rare or endangered in Vermont

Brushfoots: Admirals

Red-Spotted Admiral aka White Admiral *(Limenitis artemis artemis)* | Willow | Red-Spotted Admiral aka Red-Spotted Purple *(Limenitis artemis astyanax)* | Birch

Brushfoots: Emperors

Viceroy *(Laments archippus)* | Willow | Hackberry Emperor *(Asterocampa celtis)* critically endangered | Hackberries

Brushfoots: Fritillaries

Tawny Emperor *(Asterocampa clyton)* critically endangered | Hackberries | Aphrodite Fritillary *(Argynnis aphrodite)* | Violets

Atlantis Fritillary *(Argynnis atlantis)* | Violets | Great Spangled Fritillary *(Argynnis cybele)* | Violets

Meadow Fritillary *(Boloria bellona)* | Violets | Regal Fritillary *(Argynnis idalia)* extirpated in Vermont | Violets

Silver-bordered Fritillary
(Boloria myrina)

Violets

Variegated Fritillary
(Euptoieta claudia)
uncommon migrant

Violets

Brushfoots: Monarch

Brushfoots: Satyrs and Browns

Monarch
(Dynaus plexippus)

Milkweed

Common Ringlet
(Coenonympha california)

Grasses

Jutta Arctic
(Oeneis jutta)
critically endangered

Cotton-grass

Common Wood-Nymph
(Cercyonis pegala)

Grasses

Eyed Brown
(Lethe eurydice)

Sedges

Appalachian Brown
(Lethe appalachia)
S1S2

Grasses

Little Wood Satyr
(Megisto cymbal)

Grasses

Northern Pearly-Eye
(Lethe anthedon)

Grasses

Brushfoots: Snouts

American Snout
(*Libytheana carinenta*)
rare migrant

Hackberries

True Brushfoots: Buckeyes

Common Buckeye
(*Junonia coenia*)
rare migrant

Toadflax

True Brushfoots: Checkerspots

Baltimore Checkerspot
(*Euphydryas phaeton*)

Turtlehead

Harris' Checkerspot
(*Chlosyne harrisii*)

Asters

Silvery Checkerspot
(*Chlosyne nycteis*)
S1S2

Asters

True Brushfoots: Commas

Eastern Comma
(*Polygonia comma*)

Elm

Gray Comma
(*Polygonia progne*)

Willows

Green Comma
(*Polygonia faunus*)

Currants

True Brushfoots: Crescents

Question Mark
(*Polygonia interrogationis*)

Hackberries

Pearl Crescent
(*Phyciodes tharos*)

Asters

True Brushfoots: Ladies

Northern Crescent
(*Phyciodes cocyta*)

Asters

American Lady
(*Vanessa virginiensis*)

Pearly everlasting

Painted Lady
(*Vanessa cardui*)

Burdock

Red Admiral
(*Vanessa atalanta*)

Nettles

True Brushfoots: Tortoiseshells

Compton Tortoiseshell
(*Nymphalis l-album*)

Aspen

Milbert's Tortoiseshell
(*Aglais milberti*)

Nettles

Mourning Cloak
(*Nymphalis antiopa*)

Poplar

Brushfoots: Peacocks

European Peacock
(*Aglais io*)
introduced

Nettles

Gossamerwings: Blues / Azures

Common Blue
(*Polyommatus icarus*)
introduced

Vetch

Eastern Tailed Blue
(*Cupido comyntas*)

Clover

Gossamerwings: Blues / Azures

Summer Azure (*Celastrina neglecta*) | Dogwoods | Cherry-Gall Azure (*Celastrina serotina*) SU | Mite nipple galls on cherry leaves

Northern Azure (*Celastrina lucia*) | Dogwoods | Silvery Blue (*Glaucopsyche lygdamus*) | Legumes

Gossamerwings: Coppers

American Copper (*Lycaena hypophlaeas*) | Docks | Bronze Copper (*Lycaena hyllus*) | Docks

Bog Copper (*Tharsalea epixanthe*) critically endangered | Cranberries | Brown Elfin (*Callophrys augustinus*) S3 | Heath family

Bog Elfin (*Callophrys lanoraieensis*) SU | Black spruce | Frosted Elfin (*Callophrys irus*) S1 | Legume family

Henry's Elfin
(*Callophrys henrici*)
SU

Buckthorn

Eastern Pine Elfin
(*Callophrys niphon*)

Pines

Gossamerwings: Hairstreaks

Banded Hairstreak
(*Satyrium calanus*)

Oaks

Acadian Hairstreak
(*Satyrium acadica*)
uncommon

Willows

Early Hairstreak
(*Erora laeta*)
critically endangered

Beaked Hazelnut

Coral Hairstreak
(*Satyrium titus*)

Cherry

Gray Hairstreak
(*Strymon melinus*)
S2S3

Legumes

Edwards' Hairstreak
(*Satyrium edwardsii*)
critically endangered

Oak

Juniper Hairstreak
(*Callophrys gryneus*)
S3

Eastern Red Cedar

Hickory Hairstreak
(*Satyrium caryaevorus*)
S3

Hickory

White M Hairstreak
(*Parrhasius m-album*)
first in Vermont 2012

Oaks

Striped Hairstreak
(*Satyrium liparops*)

Many trees and shrubs

Gossamerwings: Harvester

Harvester
(*Feniseca tarquinius*)

Woolly alder aphid

Skippers: Grass Skippers

Least Skipper
(*Ancyloxypha numitor*)

Grasses

European Skipper
(*Thymelicus lineola*)
introduced

Grasses

Delaware Skipper
(*Anatrytone logan*)

Grasses

Tawny-Edged Skipper
(*Polites themistocles*)

Grasses

Crossline Skipper
(*Polites origenes*)
S3

Bluestem

Black Dash
(*Euphyes conspicua*)
critically endangered

Sedge

Dion Skipper
(*Euphyes dion*)
critically endangered

Narrow-leaved sedges

AT A GLANCE

| Dun Skipper
(*Euphyes vestris*) | Sedges | Dusted Skipper
(*Atrytonopsis hianna*)
critically endangered | Bluestem Grasses |

| Northern
Broken-Dash
(*Polites egeremet*) | Grasses | Fiery Skipper
(*Hylephila phyleus*)
uncommon vagrant | Grasses |

| Two-Spotted Skipper
(*Euphyes bimacula*)
critically endangered | Sedges | Hobomok Skipper
(*Lon hobomok*) | Grasses |

| Leonard's Skipper
(*Hesperia leonardus*) | Grasses | Little Glassywing
(*Vernia verna*) | Purpletop Grass |

| Long Dash
(*Polites mystic*) | Bluegrass | Mulberry Wing
(*Poanes massasoit*)
critically endangered | Sedge |

Common Branded Skipper
(*Hesperia comma*)
mainly Southern Vermont

Grasses

Peck's Skipper
(*Polites peckius*)

Grasses

Arctic Skipper
(*Carterocephalus mandan*)

Grasses

Broad-Winged Skipper
(*Poanes viator*)
S2S3

Grasses

Sassacus Skipper
(*Hesperia sassacus*)

Grasses

Pepper and Salt Skipper
(*Amblyscirtes hegon*)

Grasses

Skippers: Spreadwing Skippers

Common
Roadside Skipper
(*Amblyscirtes vialis*)

Grasses

Columbine Duskywing
(*Erynnis lucilius*)
SU

Columbine

Common Sootywing
(*Pholisora catullus*)
S1

Dogbane

Dreamy Duskywing
(*Erynnis icelus*)

Willow

BUTTERFLIES OF VERMONT

AT A GLANCE

Horace's Duskywing
(*Erynnis horatius*)
SU

Oaks

Juvenal's Duskywing
(*Erynnis juvenalis*)

Oaks

Northern Cloudywing
(*Thorybes pylades*)

Clover

Silver-Spotted Skipper
(*Epargyreus clarus*)

Legumes

Wild Indigo Duskywing
(*Erynnis baptisiae*)
SU

Dogbane

Common Checkered Skipper
(*Burnsius communis*)
uncommon vagrant

Grasses

Swallowtails

Canadian Tiger Swallowtail
(*Papilio canadensis*)

Birch

Eastern Giant Swallowtail
(*Papilio cresphontes*) range expanding North

Prickly Ash

Eastern Tiger Swallowtail
(*Papilio glaucus*)
S1

Birch

Spicebush Swallowtail
(*Papilio troilus*)
S1

Spicebush

Pipevine Swallowtail
(Battus philinor)
uncommon vagrant

Milkweed

Black Swallowtail
(Papilio polyxenes)

Parsley family

Whites and Yellows: Sulphurs (Yellows)

Orange Sulphur
(Colias eurytheme)

Legumes

Pink-Edged Sulphur
(Colias interior)
S3

Blueberry

Whites and Yellows: Whites

Clouded Sulphur
(Colias philodice)

Legumes

Cabbage White
(Pieris rapae)

Mustards

West Virginia White
(Pieris virginiensis)
critically endangered

Toothwort

Mustard White
(Pieris oleracea)
uncommon

Mustards

RESOURCES

The information in this guide came from the combined knowledge of many experts. There is still a lot to learn about these marvelous insects. Volunteering as a citizen scientist is a good way to assist in gaining information to help preserve butterflies in Vermont and beyond.

Books

Burns, Deborah, ed., *Xerces Society Guide to Attracting Native Pollinators*, Story Publishing, Xerces Society. 2011.

Carter, Kate. *Shrubs and Vines of Vermont*. Cotton Brook Publications. 2006.

Carter, Kate. *Wildflowers of Vermont*. Cotton Brook Publications. 2001.

Glassberg, Jeffrey. *A Swift Guide to Butterflies of North America*. Princeton University Press. 2017.

Holm, Heather. *Pollinators of Native Plants*, Pollinator Press, LLC. 2014

Scott, James. *The Butterflies of North America*. Stanford University Press. 1986.

Online Resources:

Bug Guide: A collection of experts who are willing to share their knowledge. *https://bugguide.net*

eButterfly: An online checklist and photo upload site for butterfly enthusiasts, complete with butterfly identification tool. *https://www.e-butterfly.org*

iNaturalist: A site for identifying and exploring biodiversity while generating data for scientists and environmentalists. *https://www.inaturalist.org*

McFarland K, Pfeiffer B (2022). *Vermont Butterfly Atlas 1.0 (2002-2007)*. Vermont Center for Ecostudies. Sampling event dataset https://doi.org/10.15468/y5df9j accessed via GBIF.org on 2023-02-16.

McFarland K, Pfeiffer B (2023). *Checklist of the Butterflies (Papilionoidea) of Vermont, USA*. Version 1.9. Vermont Center for Ecostudies. Checklist dataset https://doi.org/10.15468/5zrw7j accessed via GBIF.org on 2023-03-06.

Native Plant Trust: Go Botany. A useful site for New England plant identification. *https://gobotany.nativeplanttrust.org*

Vermont Center for Ecostudies: A Vermont environmental conservation and research organization. They have done great butterfly research (among other important work). *https://val.vtecostudies.org/*

Vermont Entomological Society: For those with a love of bugs and insects who like to get together with like-minded others. *https://www.vermontinsects.org/*

The Xerces Society for Invertebrate Conservation: A non-profit working to help protect invertebrates and their habitats using science informed research. *https://www.xerces.org/*

ACKNOWLEDGMENTS

Thanks to Char for laughing. Thanks to Jessie, Cyn and June for their enthusiasm for this project as well as their patience when I went on (and on) about my butterfly walks. Special thanks to Cyn and Char for their editorial eyes.

Grass Skipper

I want to thank Bryan Pfeiffer for his generosity in sharing his extensive butterfly knowledge (and for reminding me that the taxonomy of butterflies is changing fast). It was his class which got me started on this journey. I also want to thank Terri Armata for checking the butterfly photos for errors. Any mistakes are on me. Many other naturalists, and plant and butterfly enthusiasts have helped me over the years, by leading trips, answering questions, and pointing me in directions I might not have otherwise found. I'm continuously gratified by the kindness and willingness to share knowledge shown by many naturalists.

Red Admiral caterpillar (a good one)

To all my gardening friends who now send me caterpillar photos with the question: "Is this a good one?" Thanks for listening!

Unless noted below all photos in the book are my own. I'd like to thank the following people for making their photos available copyright free on *inaturalist.org*.

If there is more than one photo of the butterfly, or plant, the photo designations are tl= top left, tr= top right, bl = bottom left, br= bottom right. Cannabis: Pradip Krishen, American Cranberry: Beth Deimling, Eastern Tiger Swallowtail, Spicebush Swallowtail, Mulberry Wing, Gray Hairstreak, Little Glassywing, tr: Erik Schif, Frosted Elfin, Jutta Arctic, Hackberry Emperor, Columbine Duskywing, Two-Spotted Skipper, Early Hairstreak, West Virginia White, Harvester, tl, Crossline Skipper, Compton Tortoiseshell, Question Mark, br: Delaware Skipper, tl and tr, Banded Hairstreak, tr: Great Stinging Nettle, Greater Plaintain, Black Walnut, Butternut: Kent McFarland, American Snout: henrya, Appalachian Brown: Mike Gooley, Juniper Hairstreak: Cazody, Silvery Checkerspot: jeffcherry, Broad-Winged Skipper: Zygy, Common Buckeye, Common Hops: Kevin Keegan, Edwards' Hairstreak: mbelitz, Dion Skipper, Horace's Duskywing, Southern Cloudywing: kcthetc1, Persius Duskywing: Robb Hannawacker, Henry's Elfin: Cathy Perkins, Black Dash, Pink-Edged Sulphur: Reuven Martin, Tawny Emperor, Hickory Hairstreak: Glenn Berry, Common Sootywing, Northern Spicebush, Black Locust: Lynn Harper, Cobweb Skipper: David Eberly, Dusted Skipper: calinsdad, Bog Copper: laiet17, Bog Elfin: Naomi Cappuccino, Common Roadside Skipper, tl and tr: Ellyn Guerts, Little Glassywing, tl and br: mefisher, Leonard's Skipper, bt: Todd Eiben, Leonard's Skipper, tl: Henrique Pacheco, Leonard's Skipper, tr: Ian Whyte, Compton Tortoiseshell, tr: Sara L Giles, Compton Tortoiseshell, bl: memoosborne, Banded Hairstreak, tl: Amy Guala, Coral Hairstreak, tr: Kathleen Houlahan Chayer, Coral Hairstreak, br: forestgray, Striped Hairstreak, tl and tr: Bruce Cook, Striped Hairstreak, br, Indian Skipper, tr: Reuven Martin, Harvester, tr: Lori Schuster, Harvester, br: askalotl, Common Roadside Skipper, br: Sassacus Skipper, br: Jackson Kusack, Indian Skipper, tl: Allan Harris, Delaware Skipper, br: Kevin Keegan, Dreamy Duskywing, tr, Banded Hairstreak, br: Tracy Sherbrook, Northern Broken-Dash, rt, Early Hairstreak, Terri Armata.

If I missed anyone I apologize for the oversight.

INDEX

A
Admiral,
    Red 11, 48, 49, 52, 58
    Red-spotted 8, 11, 46, 50, 55
    White 8, 12, 45, 50, 51, 55
Aglais milberti 23, 58
    io 58
Alexander, Golden 49
Alfalfa 27, 32, 49
Amblyscirtes hegon 35, 63
Amblyscirtes vialis 35, 63
Anatrytone logan 41, 61
Ancyloxypha numitor 41, 61
Aphid 10, 16, 30, 61
Apple 50
Arctic, Jutta 9, 53, 56
Argynnis
    aphrodite 8, 13, 51, 55,
    atlantis 8, 13, 51, 55
    cybele 8, 13, 51, 55
    idalia 13, 51, 55
Aspen 7, 10, 12, 22, 44, 51
Aster 10, 18, 21, 22, 27, 33, 38, 46, 57, 58
Azure 24, 27, 48, 50
    Cherry-Gall 59
    Northern 59
    Summer 59

B
Battus phillnor 65
Bedstraw 15
Beech 46, 60
Birch 7, 11, 12, 17, 20, 22, 44, 46, 55, 64
Bird Droppings 11, 16
Blackberry 15, 26, 35, 36, 37, 38, 43
Blazing Star 38
Blue
    Common 58
    Eastern Tailed (see Tailed Blue, Eastern)
    Silvery 28, 49, 59
Blueberry 28, 30, 44, 48
Bluegrass 16, 35, 40, 41, 48
Bluestem, Big 48
Boloria
    bellona 14, 55
    myrina 14, 56
Bristlegrass 48
Broccoli 33, 49
Broken-Dash, Northern (see Skipper, Northern Broken-Dash)
Brown
    Appalachian 9, 16, 53, 56,
    Eyed 19, 16, 53, 56,
Brushfoots 1, 5, 8-24, 56-58.
Buckeye, Common 53, 57

Buckwheat 46
Burdock 46, 58
Burnsius communis 53, 64
Buttercup 26
Butternut 51, 67

C
Cabbage 31, 33
Callophrys
    augustinus 24, 25, 53, 59
    gryneus 53, 60
    henrici 53, 60
    irus 53, 59
    lanoraieensis 24, 25, 53, 59
    niphon 24, 28, 60
Cannabis 48, 67
Carrion 10, 17, 20
Carrot 6, 49
Carterocephalus mandan 36, 63
Cedar 50, 60
Celastrina
    lucia 59
    neglecta 59
    serotina 59
Cercyonis pegala 15, 56
Checkerspot
    Baltimore 5, 21, 47, 50, 57
    Harris' 21, 45, 47, 57
    Silvery 21, 47, 53, 57
Cherry 11, 12, 29, 30, 44, 50, 58, 60
Chlosyne
    harrisii 21, 57
    nycteis 21, 57
Chrysalis 2, 5
Cinquefoil 15, 27, 28, 50
Cloudywing, Northern 43, 49, 64
Clover 6, 15, 18, 26, 27, 32, 33, 36, 37, 40, 41, 42, 49, 59, 64
Coenonympha california 15, 56
Colias
    eurytheme 31, 32, 65
    interior 31, 65
    philodice 31, 32, 65
Comma
    Eastern 9, 19, 47, 48, 49, 57
    Gray 9, 19, 47, 57
    Green 9, 19, 46, 51, 57
Conservation 45, 53, 54
Cottongrass 51
Crabgrass 40
Cranberry 59
Crescent 46, 57-58
    Northern 9, 22, 58
    Pearl 9, 22, 57
Cud Weed 18
Cupido comyntas 27, 58

INDEX

Currants 19, 47, 57

D

Danaus plexippus 8, 10, 45, 46, 47, 56
Dandelion 32, 33, 44
Dill 49
Dock 26, 46, 59
Dogbane 18, 29, 30, 36, 37, 40, 43, 44, 47, 63, 64
Dogwood 27, 28, 58, 59
Dung 10, 15, 17, 19, 20, 22
Duskywing
    Columbine 43, 53, 63
    Dreamy 44, 46, 51, 53, 63
    Horace's 53, 64
    Juvenal's 44, 46, 53, 64
    Wild Indigo 43, 53, 64

E

Elfin
    Bog 24, 25, 53, 59,
    Brown 24, 25, 28, 53, 59
    Eastern Pine 24, 25, 28, 50, 59
    Frosted 24, 25, 28, 53, 59
    Henry's 24, 25, 28, 53, 60
Elm 17, 19, 20, 47, 57
Emperor
    Hackberry 9, 53, 55,
    Tawny 9, 53, 55,
Epargyreus clarus 34, 42, 64
Erora laeta 53, 60
Erynnis
    babtisae 43, 53, 64
    horatius 53, 64
    icelus 44, 46,51, 63
    juvenalis 44, 46, 53, 64
Euphydryas phaeton 21, 57
Euphyes
    conspicua 53, 61
    dion 53, 61
    vestris 39, 51, 62

F

Fennel 6
Figwort 21, 47, 57
Fir 50
Fleabane 28
Foxtails 48
Fritillary
    Aphrodite 8, 13, 51, 55
    Atlantis 8,13, 51, 55
    Great Spangled 8, 13, 51, 55
    Meadow 13, 51, 55
    Regal 13, 53, 55
    Silver-Bordered 13, 51, 56
    Variegated 13, 51, 56

Fritillaries 1, 8, 12, 13, 14, 55
Fruit 11, 12, 15, 19, 20, 22

G

Geranium 36
Glaucopsyche lygdamus 27, 59
Goldenrod 18, 30, 32
Gooseberry 19, 47
Gossamerwings 1, 5, 24-30, 58- 61.
    (See also *Lycaenidae*)
Grass
    Indian 35
    Orchard 16, 48
    Panic 40
Grasses 15, 16, 17, 35, 36, 37, 38, 39, 40, 41, 42, 56, 61, 62

H

Hackberry 11, 17, 20, 47, 48, 55, 57, 67
Hairstreak
    Acadian 60
    Banded 25, 29, 51, 60
    Coral 25, 29, 51, 60
    Early 53, 60
    Edwards 53, 60
    Gray 53, 60
    Hickory 53, 60
    Juniper 53, 60
    Striped 25, 30,48, 50, 61
    White M 61
Harvester 30, 46, 61
Hawkweed 15, 42
Hazelnut 46, 60
Heath 47, 48, 59
Hemlock 50
Hemp 11, 47, 48
Heraclides cresphontes 7, 64
Hesperia leonardus 38, 62,
    sassacus 38, 63
Hesperiidae (See Skippers)
Hickory 29, 51, 60, 67
Hophornbeam 46
Hops 11, 19, 48, 67
Host Plants 2, 5, 45, 46, 47, 48, 49, 50, 51, 52

I

Invasive Plants 4, 52
Iris 36

J

Joe-pyed Weed 10, 12, 13, 14

L

Labrador Tea 48
Lady, American 18, 23, 45, 46, 58
    Painted 18, 46, 48, 49, 58

INDEX

Leatherleaf 48
Legume 18, 28, 32, 42, 43, 58, 59, 64, 65
Lepidoptera 4
Lethe
 anthedon 17, 48, 56,
 appalachia 9, 16, 53, 56
 eurydice 9, 16, 51, 56
Libytheana carinenta 31, 32, 49, 57
Lilac 10
Limenitis
 archippus 10, 55
 arthemis arthemis 12, 55
 arthemis astyanax 11, 55
Locust 42, 51, 67
Lon hobomok 37, 62
Lupine 18, 43, 44, 49
Lycaena
 hyllus 24, 26, 59
 hypophlaeas 24, 26, 55–73, 59
Lycaenidae (See Gossamerwing)

M

Mallow 18, 48
Meadowsweet 27
Megisto cymela 16, 48, 56
Metalmarks (*Riodinidae*) 1
Milkweed 6, 10, 12, 13, 14, 18, 28, 29, 30, 32,
 36, 37, 39, 40, 41, 42, 45, 47
Mint 33, 41
Monarch 8, 10, 45, 47, 56
Mourning Cloak 17,46, 47, 48, 51, 58
Mullein 47
Mustard 31, 33, 49, 65

N

Nettle 11, 19, 20, 23, 49, 58, 67
New Jersey Tea 27, 29, 30, 43, 44
Ninebark 50
Nutgrass 41
Nymphalidae (see Brushfoot)
Nymphalis
 antiopa 17, 58
 l-album 22, 58

O

Oak 11, 29, 36, 44, 46, 60, 64

P

Pansy 51
Papilio
 canadensis 6, 7, 64
 glaucus 6, 64
 polyxenes 6, 65
 troilus 6, 64
Papilionidae (See Swallowtail)
Parrhasius m-album 61

Parsley 6, 49, 64
Peacock, European 58
Pearly everlasting 18, 46, 58
Pearly-Eye, Northern 17, 48, 56
Pesticides 52
Phlox 38
Phyciodes
 sp. 9, 22, 46, 57-58
 tharos 22, 57
 cocyta 22, 58
Pieridae (See Whites and Yellows)
Pieris
 oleracea 31, 33, 65
 rapae 31, 33, 65
 virginiensis 31, 65
Pine 24, 25, 28, 50, 59
Plantain 50
Plum 29, 50
Poanes viator 53, 63
Polites
 egeremet 40, 63
 mystic 37, 62
 origenes 61
 peckius 36, 63
 themistocles 40, 61
Polygonia
 comma 19, 57
 faunus 20, 57
 interrogationis 20, 57
 progne 19, 57
Polyommatus icarus 58
Poplar 10, 11, 12, 17, 51
Puddling 2
Pupa 5
Purpletop 39, 61
Pussytoes 18, 46, 58

Q

Queen Anne's Lace 6, 49
Question Mark 9, 20, 47, 48, 49, 50, 57

R

Ringlet, Common 15, 16, 48, 50, 51, 56
Rose 50
Rushes 15, 50

S

Sap 11, 12, 16, 17, 19, 22, 30
Satyr, Little Wood 16, 48, 56
Satyrium
 acadicum 60
 calanus 25, 29, 60
 edwardsii 60
 iparops 25, 30, 60
 titus 25, 29, 60
Sedge 15, 16, 39, 41, 51, 56, 61, 62, 63

INDEX

Selfheal 35
Skipper
    Arctic 36, 63
    Black Dash 53, 61
    Broad-Winged 53, 63
    Common Branded 63
    Common Checkered 53, 64
    Common Roadside 35, 63
    Crossline 53, 61
    Delaware 41, 51, 61
    Dion 53, 61
    Dun 39, 51, 62
    Dusted 53, 62
    European 42, 61
    Fiery 62
    Hobomok 37, 62
    Indian (see Sassacus)
    Least 41, 61
    Leonard's 38, 62
    Little Glassywing 39, 62
    Long Dash 37, 62
    Mullberry wing 53, 62
    Northern Broken-Dash 40, 62
    Peck's 36, 63
    Pepper and Salt 35, 63
    Sassacus 38, 63
    Silver-Spotted 34, 42, 49, 64
    Tawny-Edged 40, 61
    Two-Spotted 62
Skippers 1, 34-44, 51
Smartweed 46
Snapdragon 50
Snout, American 9, 57
Sootywing, Common 53, 63
Sorrel 26, 41, 46, 59
Speedwell 50
Spicebush 6, 64, 67
Spruce 50, 59
Steeplebush 50
Strawberry 28
Strymon melinus 53, 60
Sulphur
    Clouded 31, 32, 49, 65
    Orange 31, 32, 49, 65
    Pink-Edged 31, 32, 49, 65
Swallowtail
    Black 6, 49, 65
    Canadian Tiger 7, 46, 50, 64
    Eastern Giant 6, 64
    Eastern Tiger 7, 51, 53, 64
    Pipevine 6, 65
    Spicebush 6, 53, 64
Swallowtails 1, 4, 6-7, 64-65

T
Tailed Blue, Eastern 27, 49, 58

Teaberry, Eastern 48
Tharsalea epixanthe 24, 59
Thistle 18, 38, 40, 41, 42, 43
Thorybes pylades 43, 64
Thymelicus lineola 42, 63
Timothy 42, 48
Toadflax 50, 57
Toothwort 49, 65
Tortoiseshell
    Compton 22, 46, 51, 58
    Milbert's 23, 49, 58
Trefoil 42, 49
Turtlehead 21, 47

V
Vanessa
    atalanta 8, 11, 58
    cardui 18, 58
    virginiensis 18, 58
Verbena 35, 41
Vernia verna 39, 53, 62
Vetch 27, 28, 40, 42, 43, 49
Viburnum 35
Viceroy 8, 10, 51, 55
Violet 12, 13, 14, 51, 55, 56

W
Walnut 29, 51, 67
White
    Cabbage 65
    Mustard 65
    West Virginia 65
Whites and Yellows 1, 5, 31-32, 65
Wild Indigo 43, 64
Willow 10, 11, 12, 17, 20, 22, 44, 51, 55, 57, 60, 63
Wintercress 49
Wisteria 44
Wood-Nymph, Common 15, 48, 56

Y
Yarrow 27

BUTTERFLIES OF VERMONT